# Religious Topics

# FEASTING AND FASTING

Jon Mayled

Wayland

## Religious Topics

Art and Architecture    Initiation Rites
Birth Customs           Marriage Customs
Death Customs           Pilgrimage
Family Life             Religious Dress
Feasting and Fasting    Religious Services
Holy Books              Teachers and Prophets

**Cover** *Muslims eating* Suhur, *the light meal which they take before dawn during the month of* Ramadan.

First published in 1986 by Wayland (Publishers) Limited
61 Western Road, Hove, East Sussex BN3 1JD, England

British Library Cataloguing in Publication Data
Mayled, Jon
   Feasting and Fasting. (Religious Topics)
   1. Fasts and feasts
   I. Title     II. Series
   291.4′46              BL590
   ISBN 0–85078–769–6

Phototypeset by Kalligraphics Ltd., Redhill, Surrey
Printed in Italy by G. Canale & C.S.p.A., Turin
Bound in the U.K. at The Bath Press, Avon

# Contents

# Introduction

There are many reasons why we have feasts. We have feasts because we are happy and to celebrate special events, and we have them when all our friends and family are together. If you do not eat food for some time then this could be called fasting. Most of us do not eat

*Feasting is a time to celebrate with family and friends.*

food during the night and this is why the first meal of the day is called breakfast – 'breaking-fast'.

Many religions celebrate very important religious events with a feast. Often, the feast follows a period of fasting.

Fasting can mean different things to each religion but it is important to all of them, to prepare people for the feast. Some people fast to remind themselves of the sufferings of their god. Others fast so as to know what it is like to be without food and luxuries and so remember to thank God for all they have. Some people fast to remind themselves of the hunger and need of poor people. Some people fast to show God they are sorry for any sins they have committed and to show that they will try to lead better lives in the future.

In each case fasting ensures that when the time comes for the feast it will be much more enjoyable.

*Fasting is not a strict rule in the Buddhist religion.*

# Buddhism

Fasting is not a strict rule in the Buddhist religion. Monks, however, eat only one meal a day, around midday, and must eat whatever

*Buddhist monks eat whatever food is offered to them.*

is offered to them. However, in Thailand, where nearly everyone follows a form of Buddhism called *Theravāda*, there is a period during the rainy season when for three months from July onwards the monks *(Sangha)* go into retreat. People give them special offerings and no weddings or festivals take place. These three months mark the time when it is believed that the Buddha went to heaven and preached to the gods.

This period ends with a great full moon festival. All the houses and temples are lit up to celebrate the Buddha's return and the monks are given new clothes.

The most important Buddhist feast in Thailand, Sri Lanka and many other Buddhist countries is *Wesak*. This usually takes place in May. During *Wesak*, the streets and houses are decorated and there are processions. Presents are given to the poor and to the monks. This festival celebrates three important

*Buddhists try to lead good lives by not causing suffering to others.*

events in the life of the Buddha: his birth; the moment when he learnt the truth about life and the suffering it involves; and the time when he left earth and reached *Nirvāna*, the final escape from suffering.

*The most important feast in many Buddhist countries is* Wesak.

# Christianity

Feasting and fasting customs have changed over the years for Christians and they differ amongst Christians who belong to different churches or groups.

Many Christians, especially Catholics, choose not to eat meat on Fridays. This is in memory of the Friday that Jesus died on the cross.

The main period of fasting for Christians is the forty days of Lent which lead up to the festival of Easter. In the past many Christians ate only one meal a day during Lent so as to concentrate on prayer, and as preparation for Easter when they remember the death and resurrection of Jesus.

Lent begins in February, on Ash Wednesday. The day before is known as Shrove Tuesday or Pancake Tuesday. In the past Christians used to eat pancakes on this day so as

*Many Christians choose not to eat meat on Fridays, as it was on a Friday that Jesus died on the cross.*

9

*A procession during Holy Week in Brazil.*

to use up all the eggs and butter. In those days these foods were forbidden during Lent. Pancake Tuesday is an opportunity to feast before the fast.

Today many Christians usually try to do without one luxury, perhaps sweets or chocolate, during Lent. The money saved is sometimes sent to charities.

The last week of Lent is called Holy Week, and during this time Christians read about and remember the events of the last weeks of Jesus' life. Jesus was crucified on Good Friday, and nowadays Christians eat Hot Cross Buns on Good Friday in memory of His death. Some churches remember His death by hanging up purple cloths and not lighting the candles on this day.

At midnight on the next day, Easter Saturday, there are great celebrations. The churches are filled with music, bells, candles and flowers. It was on Easter Day that His

*At Easter, Christians celebrate with special meals and chocolate Easter eggs.*

disciples saw Jesus and knew that He had come back to life. Because of this, Easter is the most important feast day of the Christian year. Many people celebrate with special meals and give presents. In the weeks before Easter the shops sell Easter eggs and chocolate figures of chickens and rabbits.

Jesus coming back from the dead was a very important event for Christians, as it showed how He had overcome death. The eggs and chickens represent new life. They also connect Easter with much older feasts that

*At Christmas, Christians decorate their homes and eat special food.*

were held to celebrate the end of winter and the new life which comes with spring.

The other important Christian feast is Christmas, the traditional birthday of Jesus. People celebrate by giving presents and sending cards. In some countries, Christians decorate their homes with Christmas trees and eat special food such as Christmas pudding, Christmas cake, and turkey or goose. For all Christians Christmas is a time for celebration.

# Hinduism

Hinduism is a religion which has many feast days. Religious events are celebrated with special foods and ceremonies.

The birthday of Lord Krishna, an important Hindu god, is called *Janamashtami*, and takes place in autumn. The day before the event people fast to prepare themselves for the celebration. At midnight bells are rung and in the temple conch shells are blown. In the temple, there is a statue of the baby Krishna in a cradle covered with flowers. Worshippers offer sweetmeats to Krishna which are then shared among the congregation. All night the worshippers stay in the temple, singing.

A birthday feast is also held for the god, Lord Rama, called *Ram Navami*. It is a fast day and worshippers cannot eat cereals, salt or everyday vegetables. Instead they

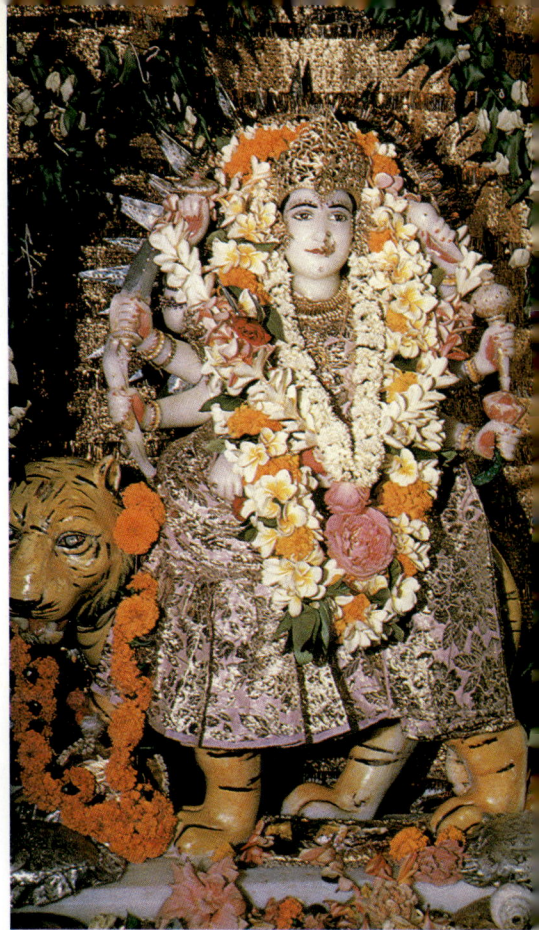

*At festival times Hindus decorate their homes and shrines with garlands of flowers.*

13

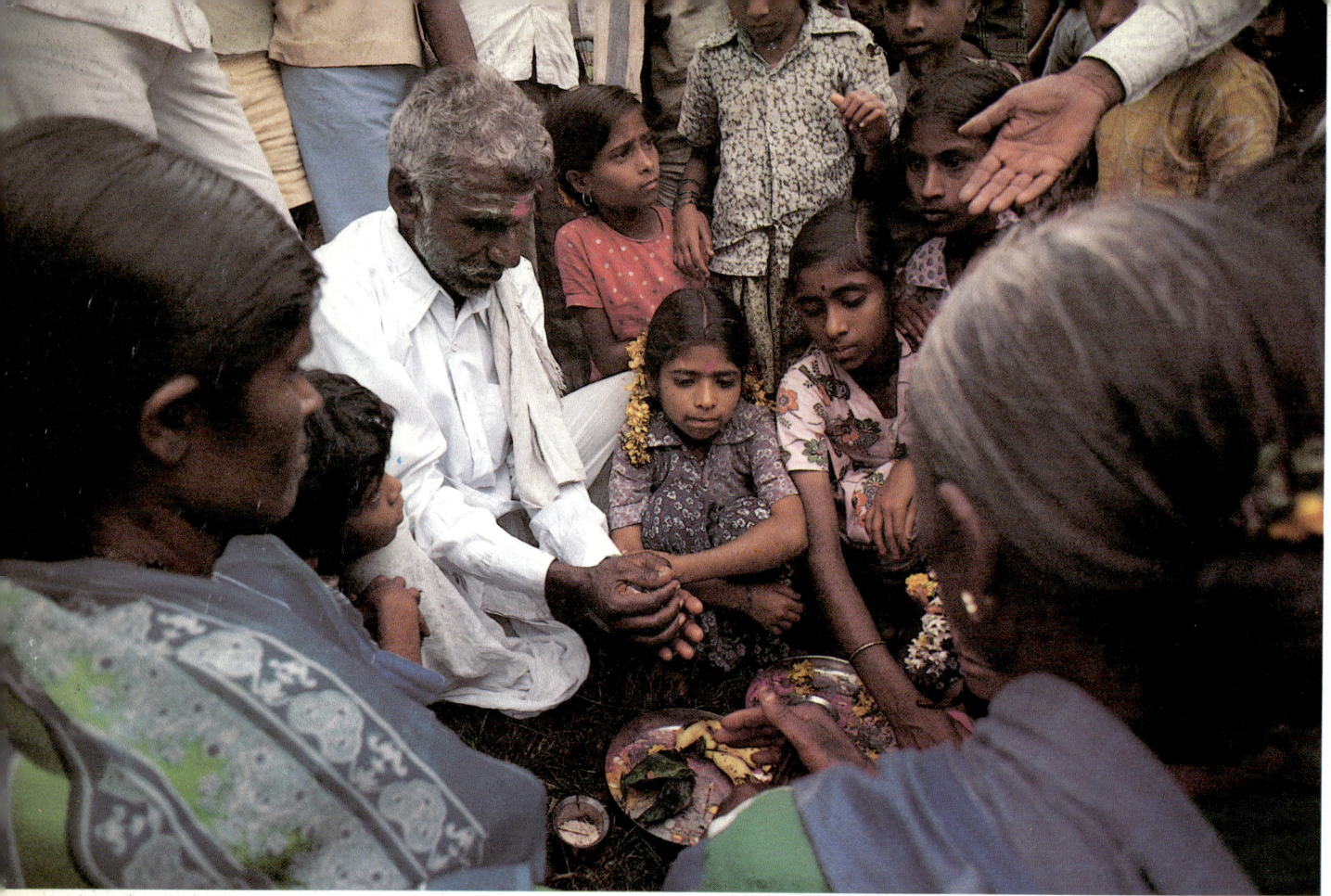

*A Hindu religious ceremony in Mysore.*

celebrate with special foods. In the temple the hundred names of Rama are sung and stories about him are read all through the day and night.

Another important feast day is *Diwali*

*Annakoot*. This is the day after the festival of *Diwali*. According to legend, on this day thousands of years ago, it rained so much that

*A Hindu religious teacher.*

15

*This Hindu family is celebrating the festival of* Diwali.

the people of India almost drowned. In order to save them, Krishna picked up the Govardhana Mountain and held it over their heads like an umbrella until the rains stopped. In return they cooked food and gave it to him. Now the food is offered to Krishna and then shared among the congregation.

# Islam

Fasting, or *Sawm* is a very important part of Muslim religion. Every healthy Muslim must fast between daybreak and sunset during the Islamic month of *Ramadan*. This is ordered by the *Qur'an*, the Muslim holy book.

*These children are learning the* Qur'an, *which is the Muslim holy book.*

*A Muslim family outside their house in Poona, India.*

*Ramadan* was the month when the *Qur'an* was first given to the Prophet Muhammad who was the founder of Islam. Muslims fast at this time to show they can do without food for long periods of time, and so prove they can follow the will of Allah.

As well as fasting, every Muslim who can afford to, is asked to donate money. This is to acknowledge the pain and needs of the poor.

During *Ramadan* Muslims say special prayers and go to extra services at the mosque.

The Muslim calendar differs from the one used in Christian countries like Britain and America, and *Ramadan* occurs at a different time every year. This means that sometimes the daylight hours can be short, as they are in winter, while in other years they are very long, as *Ramadan* falls during the summer months. Each new month, including

*Ramadan*, begins with the appearance of the new moon.

When the next new moon is visible, *Ramadan* is over and the month of *Shawwal* begins. On the first day of *Shawwal* is the feast of *Id ul-Fitr*, 'the festival of fast breaking'. Many Muslims gather at the mosque for special prayers and a sermon is given to mark the

*A Muslim family having* Iftar, *the evening meal which is taken after sundown during* Ramadan.

*Muslims celebrate the feast of* Id ul-Fitr, *which is 'the festival of fast breaking'.*

end of *Ramadan*. All day Muslims greet each other saying,

'*Id Mubarak* (Blessings and joy of '*Id*).

Before they go to the '*Id* prayers, everyone takes a bath and puts on new clothes. Families and friends visit one another and send each other cards. People eat special food and sweets to celebrate the festival. Muslims also give enough money or food for one extra meal, so that the poor people in their community can also feast and celebrate the festival.

20

# Judaism

For Jews there is one important day of fasting in the year. This occurs on the most holy day of *Yom Kippur*, or the 'Day of Atonement'. *Yom Kippur* comes at the end of a period called 'The Ten Days of Repentance' – a time occurring around September when Jews

*A rabbi holding the* Torah *scroll, which contains the first five books of the Holy Scriptures.*

*Moses freed the Jews from slavery in Egypt.*

remember all the things they have done wrong during the past year, and promise to do better in the future.

During *Yom Kippur*, no work is done, no food is eaten, nor liquid drunk. People do not wear leather shoes or make-up and do not have a bath. Keeping these rules makes it a very special day when Jews can concentrate on the past year and the new one which is a about to begin.

At the afternoon service in the synagogue, Jews listen to the book of Jonah which is read from the *Tenakh* (the Jewish holy scripture). The readings remind the congregation that however ordinary and weak people are, they still have a job to do in the community for God. At the end of the evening service, a ram's-horn trumpet called a *shofar* is blown to show that the old year is finally over.

There are many special festivals and feasts in Jewish worship, but the most popular and special is the *Passover* festival. The first night of *Passover (Pesach)* is known as *Seder* night. The word *Seder* means 'order', and the whole ceremony is arranged in a special order of events. The *Passover* festival celebrates the time when the Jewish people were released from slavery in Egypt by Moses.

*These people are celebrating* Passover *around a* Seder *table.*

23

*The* Sabbath *feast begins with the blessing of wine and bread.*

Preparations for the festival begin weeks before, when houses are cleaned from top to bottom. This is to ensure that no leaven — food which contains yeast, such as bread — will be found in the house by the time the festival arrives.

When the festival begins special dishes and cutlery, which are used only for the *Passover* meal are put on the *Seder* table. Each has a copy of a special book called the *Haggadah*. All the items to be eaten have special meanings which refer to the freeing of the Jews. Even the cushions on the chairs are a symbol of freedom.

Another important festival in Jewish worship is the *Sabbath* feast, or *Shabbat*, which takes place every Saturday. The *Sabbath* is a time for prayer and to think about God. On Friday evening, which is the beginning of the *Sabbath*, there is a short service at the synagogue, followed by the evening meal.

*The* Havdalah *service marks the end of the* Sabbath.

This is a large and special feast which begins with the wine and specially braided bread being blessed.

On Saturday there is a morning service at the synagogue and at lunchtime Jews sometimes eat a stew called *cholent*.

The *Sabbath* ends with the *Havdalah* service. At the end of the service wine is passed around and everyone greets each other with:

*Shavuah tov* – 'a good week'.

25

# Sikhism

Sikhs do not fast as part of their religious duties. They do not believe that doing without food for a particular day can bring them any nearer to God.

Feasting, however, is an important part of their religion. In each *Gurdwara*, or temple, there is the *Guru ka langar*, the Guru's

*The* Akal Takt *is the centre of Sikh religious and social learning.*

*These Sikh women are preparing food in the* Guru ka langar, *the Guru's kitchen.*

kitchen. Here, when prayers are over, everyone, whether they are rich or poor, sits down and eats together.

Sikhs celebrate three special festivals, called *Gurpurbs*, during the year. These are the birthdays of the first and the tenth Gurus, Guru Nanak and Guru Gobind Singh, and the day on which the fifth guru, Guru Arjan, died.

So that as many people as possible can attend, the *Gurpurb* is celebrated on the first weekend after the date of the anniversary.

At every *Gurpurb* the whole of the Sikh holy book, the *Guru Granth Sahib*, is read. This reading is called the *Akhand Path* and lasts about forty-eight hours, finishing on Sunday morning.

When the reading is over the service, *Diwan*, reminds people about the particular Guru whose anniversary is being celebrated.

*An* Akhand Path, *a continuous reading of the* Guru Granth Sahib.

*After* Diwan, *Sikhs welcome anyone who wishes to stay for the festival* langar *or meal.*

After *Diwan* Sikhs welcome anyone who wishes to stay for the *Langar* or meal.

Sikhs believe that they should share their celebrations and feasts with everyone from whatever religion, and twice each day a congregational prayer is said in the *Gurdwara*, which ends by asking God that:

> *'By Thy Infinite Grace and Sweet Will, May the whole of Humankind be blessed.'*

# Glossary

**Allah** The Muslim name for God.

**Buddha** Meaning the 'Awakened One'. The Buddha was *Siddhartha Gautama*, the son of an Indian King who lived about 4,500 years ago. *Gautama* gave up all his wealth in order to dedicate himself to following a religious life.

**Disciples** The men chosen by Jesus to help Him spread the word of God.

**Guru** 'Teacher'. The name given to the ten human leaders of the Sikh religion.

**Jesus** The son of God.

**Langar** The name for the kitchen and the food which is prepared and eaten at the *Gurdwara* after a service.

**Lord Krishna** A Hindu god.

**Lord Rama** A Hindu god.

**Mosque** Muslim place of worship.

**Muhammad** The great Muslim prophet and founder of Islam.

**Nirvāna** The aim of all Buddhists. It is the transformation of all personal desires into wisdom and compassion.

**Synagogue** A Jewish place of worship.

# Further Reading

If you would like to find out more about feasting and fasting, you may like to read the following books:

*Beliefs and Believers* series – published by Wayland.
*Exploring Religion* series – published by Bell and Hyman.
*Festivals* series – published by Wayland.

*Religions of the World* series – published by Wayland.
*Worship* series – published by Holt-Saunders.

The following videos are very helpful:
*Through the Eyes* series – produced by CEM Video, 2 Chester House, Pages Lane, London N10.

# Acknowledgements

The Publisher would like to thank the following for providing the pictures for this book: Bruce Coleman 11, 14; Camerapix Hutchison Library 8, 16, 17; Christine Osborne COVER, 4, 19; Colorpix 15, 18, 26; John Topham 10, 12; Mary Evans 9, 22; Outlook Films Limited 13, 28; Sally and Richard Greenhill 29; Susan Griggs 20; Zefa 5, 6, 7, 21, 23, 24, 25.

# Index